Eastern Angles and
present

I CAUGHT CRABS IN WALBERSWICK

by **Joel Horwood**

ONE	Andrew Barron
TWO	Rosie Thomson
WHEELER	Harry Hepple
FITZ	Aaron Foy
DANI	Gemma Soul
Director	Lucy Kerbel
Designer	takis
Lighting Designer	Matt Prentice
Sound Designer	Steve Mayo
Movement	Shona Morris
Dramaturgy	Beth Byrne
Production Manager	Steve Cooney
Company Stage Manager (Edinburgh and tour)	Penny Griffin
Company Stage Manager (The Bush)	Louise Cable
Associate Sound Designer	Luke Swaffield

**1 – 5 May 2008 HIGHTIDE FESTIVAL
at The Cut, Halesworth**
Performed by Paul Trussell, Judith Scott, David Hartley, Joseph Arkley and
Matti Houghton, with Emma McKie as Stage Manager

**1 – 25 August 2008 PLEASANCE COURTYARD
as part of the Edinburgh Festival Fringe**

3 – 11 October 2008 on tour

11 November – 6 December 2008 THE BUSH THEATRE, London

The **Company**

Andrew Barron ONE

Andrew trained at East 15 Acting School. He has received critical acclaim for his one-man show *Up The Gary* which has toured festivals and theatres throughout the country including the Edinburgh Festival Fringe (Underbelly) and New York Fringe. Andrew also won the Michael MacLiammoir Award for Best Actor at the Dublin International Gay Theatre Festival for his performance in *All Alone*. Other theatre credits include: *The Whale and the Bird* (Theatre503); *Terrorist – The Musical* (Theatre503, Underbelly); *American Shorts* (Kings Head); *Asylum Monologues* (Wooden Hill). Andrew has also appeared as Mark Dixie in the BBC drama-documentary film *The Murder of Sally Anne Bowman* and clocked up a good number of commercials including Churchill Insurance, the *Guardian*, Astra and Sky. He was also recently featured as an ident for Tic Tac Mints around the popular programme *My Name is Earl*.

Beth Byrne Dramaturgy

Beth studied English and Theatre at Leeds University and began work at London's Bridewell Theatre as Assistant Administrator. After working in the ACE Drama Dept, she was headhunted for the Donmar Warehouse and promoted internally to become their Production Administrator and Literary Manager where she curated their new-writing seasons, notably productions of *Take Me Out*, *Proof* and *Lobby Hero*. When Sam Mendes and Caro Newling formed Neal Street Productions in 2003, Beth joined the theatre arm as Producer, dealing with their commissions, their dramaturgy and co-producing their productions, most recently the Peepolykus production of *The Hound of the Baskervilles* at the Duchess, Samuel Adamson's adaptation of Almodovar's *All About my Mother* at the Old Vic and forthcoming productions of commissioned plays *To Be Or Not To Be* by Nick Whitby on Broadway fall '08, *The House of Special Purpose* by Heidi Thomas scheduled for Chichester '09 and *The Bridge Project*, a transatlantic collaboration between Brooklyn Academy of Music and the Old Vic in '09.

Louise Cable Company Stage Manager (The Bush)

Louise studied History of Art at Manchester University before changing her mind completely and applying to drama school. She trained as a stage manager at the Royal Academy of Dramatic Art and since graduating has been working in Australia with the Sydney Theatre Company. Her shows with the STC include *Waikiki Hip*, *Tales from the Vienna Woods* and *The Vertical Hour*. Her work in the UK includes *Sh*t M*x* at Trafalgar Studios and *The 39 Steps*. Louise is thrilled to be joining Eastern Angles on this exciting project.

Aaron Foy FITZ

Aaron trained at East 15 School of Acting. At East 15 theatre includes: Tom in *Citizenship*, Jeff in *Aforenightcome* and Snake in *The School for Scandal*.

Harry Hepple WHEELER

Theatre includes: *The Wizard of Oz* (Birmingham Rep, dir. Rachel Kavanagh); *Alaska* (Royal Court, dir. Maria Aberg); *Toast* (Royal Court, dir. Richard Wilson); *Exposure* (workshop, dir. David Newman); *Donnington Castle* (Nabokov, Present:Tense); *Been So Long* (workshop, Young Vic, dir. Che Walker and Arthur Darvill); *Drywrite*. Short film includes: *Clean* (Rehab Films, dir. David Ganly); *A Day in the Life* (HaWay Productions, dir. Louis Weirs). Radio includes: *The Two Gentlemen of Verona* (dir. Jonathan Tafler).

Joel Horwood Writer

Mikey The Pikey (the musical) won the Cameron Mackintosh Award and subsequently enjoyed a sell-out run at the Pleasance during the 2005 Edinburgh Festival Fringe. His second play *Cattleprod Shakedown* (Stephen Joseph Theatre) earned Joel a place on the Royal Court and BBC 'The 50' initiative for promising writers. *Food* (Fringe First award-winner) and *Stoopud Fucken Animals* played at the Traverse Theatre in 2006 and 2007 respectively. *Ok Computer* (an adaptation of the Radiohead album) aired on the BBC's *The Wire*, *The Dogs* (Heat and Light) played the Hampstead Theatre in July and *Public Displays of Affection* ran at this year's Latitude Festival. Joel is currently under commission from the the West Yorkshire Playhouse and is the Arts Council East's writer-in-residence with Nabokov and the Watford Palace Theatre.

Lucy Kerbel Director

Directing includes: *I Am a Superhero* (Old Vic New Voices/Theatre503); *Twelfth Night*, *Much Ado About Nothing*, *Romeo and Juliet* (Sprite Productions, Ripley Castle); *Mouse* (Underbelly); *Is Everyone OK?* (Nabokov, Latitude Festival); *East is East* (extracts, Royal Court); *Guy Fawkes Night* (Old Vic New Voices 24 Hour Plays); *Love and Money* (Young Vic Shorts). Work as an assistant director includes: *Attempts On Her Life*, *Waves* (National Theatre); *Intemperance* (Liverpool Everyman); *Hamlet* (English Touring Theatre, national tour and West End); *Bone* (Royal Court). Lucy was the recipient of the 2005/6 Cohen Directors Bursary at the National Theatre Studio and English Touring Theatre. She was a joint winner of the 2007 Old Vic New Voices 503 Award.

Steve Mayo Sound Designer

Sound designs include: *Sh*t M*x*, *Snowbound* (Trafalgar Studios); *Fight Face* (Lyric Studio); *I Caught Crabs in Walberswick*, *Lie of the Land*, *Lough/Rain* (Edinburgh Festival Fringe 2008); *Hangover Square*, *Eden's Empire* (Finborough); *Absolutely Frank* (Queen's, Hornchurch); *Stovepipe*, *I Caught Crabs in Walberswick* (HighTide Festival 2008); *Jack and the Beanstalk* (Barbican); *Romeo and Juliet* (BAC); *Future/Perfect* (Soho); *Weightless*, *You Were After Poetry*, *Lyre*, *Ned & Sharon* (HighTide Festival 2007). For more information visit www.steve-mayo.co.uk.

Shona Morris Movement

Movement directing includes: *As You Like It*, *An English Tragedy* (Watford Palace); *The Tempest* (Sibelius at the Barbican); *The Guns of Carrar*, *Le Grand Meaulnes* (Cochrane); *Swine* (workshop, National Theatre Studio); *Twelfth Night* (Chichester Festival Theatre); *Nicholas Nickleby* (Chichester Festival Theatre, West End tour, Gielgud, Toronto); *Scenes from the Back of Beyond* (Royal Court); *Lost Tourists* (site-specific physical theatre piece, Pompidou Centre, Paris); *Oedipus Rex* (Greek Society at the Cambridge Arts Theatre); *The Tempest* (Liverpool Playhouse); *Hamlet* (West Yorkshire Playhouse); *Frankenstein, Early Morning* (National Theatre Studio). Shona has also worked as Movement Coach and Movement Director at the Stratford Festival Theatre, Canada, where work included: *Agamemnon*, *The Flies*, *Electra*, *The Birds* (Greek Season), *Henry VIII*, *King Lear*, *Antony and Cleopatra*.

Matt Prentice Lighting Designer

Matt started life in theatre as a trainee lighting designer and production electrician at the Bristol Old Vic Theatre Royal. During his three-year apprenticeship he worked on all the main-house shows in the Theatre Royal and on productions in the New Vic Studio. After finishing his apprenticeship, he continued to work at the Bristol Old Vic as Lighting Designer and Production Electrician. After a few years of freelancing, Matt joined

Mountview Academy of Theatre Arts, first as a Lighting Tutor and then became Head of Lighting Design. In January 2006 Matt moved to the Royal Academy of Dramatic Art as Head of Lighting. Recent freelance work includes: the UK premiere of *Parade the Musical* (South Side, Edinburgh); *A Chorus Line* (Shaw Theatre); *The House of Bernarda Alba* (Players Theatre); The Young People's Theatre Company Showcase (Gielgud); *Faust* (Punchdrunk/National Theatre); *Peter Pan* (Assembly Room, Derby); *Masque of the Red Death* (Punchdrunk, BAC). Matt was Lighting Designer for the HighTide Festival 2008, and won the Critics' Circle Award for Best Production Design 2006 for *Faust*.

Gemma Soul DANI

Gemma is a recent graduate from Guildhall School of Music and Drama. Theatre while training includes: Irina in *Three Sisters*, Flipanta in *The Confederancy*, Chorus in *Medea*, Gwendolin in *The Importance of Being Earnest*, Sally in *House and Garden*; Georgie in *The Full Monty*, Ophelia in *Hamlet*, Mopsa/Dion in *The Winter's Tale*, Peggy in *The London Cuckolds*, Dorcas in *Plenty*, Dolly in *Etta Jenks*, and Tanis Marshall in *Semi-Monde* (dir. Alistair McGowan).

takis Designer

takis studied Stage Design at the Romanian National University of Arts and on the RADA Theatre Technical Arts Course, graduating with Distinction in 2004. Currently he is undertaking a practice-based PhD at the London College of Fashion. He has worked as Model Room Assistant at the Royal Opera House, as Scenic Art Assistant at the Greek National Opera and as Costume Assistant for the Opera Festival of Rome. He has been a guest lecturer and workshop leader at the Romanian National University of Arts in Bucharest, the Royal Academy of Dramatic Art, where he is leading the Theatre Design Summer Course, and the Lyric Hammersmith with its Lyric Young Company. His work has been seen in around forty-five worldwide productions in various indoor and outdoor venues.

Rosie Thomson TWO

Since graduating from the Drama Centre, theatre includes: *Henna Night* (Chelsea Theatre); *The Hot House* (Lyttelton Theatre). Television includes: *Family Affairs*, *The Bill*, *Second Sight*, *Dream Team*, *A Touch of Frost*, *Judge John Deed*, *EastEnders*. Film includes: *Enigma* Rosie has worked extensively with The Apathists at Theatre503, Southwark Playhouse and the Union Theatre, and is a founder member of the Operating Theatre Company.

Eastern Angles gratefully acknowledges the support of
The Peggy Ramsay Foundation
and Suffolk, Norfolk and Essex County Councils.

Since 1982 Eastern Angles has created work with a sense of place and then presented it locally, regionally and nationally. Eastern Angles collaborates with companies across the country, producing original productions for touring to a wide range of venues, especially in rural areas.

This production of *I Caught Crabs in Walberswick* was commissioned following Joel's play *Stoopud Fucken Animals*, which appeared at the Traverse during the 2007 Edinburgh Festival Fringe. It was previewed at Suffolk's HighTide Festival in May 2008 before going to Edinburgh in August and then on a tour to schools, colleges and theatres in early autumn.

The company has just finished a week-long residency in East Anglia with British-African theatre company Tiata Fahodzi, taking its production of two short plays, *Tiata Delights 08*, premiered at the Almeida, to the eastern region during African History Month.

This autumn we will be starting out on a landmark project, *Platform Peterborough*, to produce new work and engage with audiences in the new communities of one of the East of England's largest growth areas, Peterborough.

Following our Christmas production, *The Haunted Commode* by Julian Harries and Pat Whymark, we will be touring to town and village halls with *Return to Akenfield* by Craig Taylor, a twenty-first-century re-examination of Ronald Blythe's famous Suffolk village, looking at how life has been changed by incomers, supermarkets and farmworkers from all corners of the new Europe.

Also in the pipeline is a new play, *Martyrs* by Alastair Cording, about St Edmund and the fall of the Berlin Wall, and a site-specific piece, *Bentwater Roads* by Tony Ramsay, which explores the stories behind a landscape.

We will also be staging a re-tour of our summer production of Arthur Ransome's *We Didn't Mean to Go to Sea*, adapted by Nick Wood.

For Eastern Angles

Artistic Director	Ivan Cutting
General Manager	Jill Streatfeild
Marketing Officer	Karen Goddard
Production Manager	Steve Cooney
Company Stage Manager	Penny Griffin
Administrator	Carla Firman
Theatre and Outreach Manager	Jon Tavener
Box Office	Hazel Hicks

If you are interested in working in partnership with Eastern Angles to make and deliver exciting new theatre contact us on **01473 218202** or email **admin@easternangles.co.uk**
www.easternangles.co.uk

'HighTide's hands-on approach reminds us that a play is the sum of all the investment in it.' Financial Times

HighTide exists to source, develop and produce the best new work by emerging playwrights.

The third annual HighTide Festival will take place in Suffolk from 29 April – 10 May 2009. Tickets go on sale on 1 March 2009.

'HighTide is an important and effective company for staging new works.' Nicholas Hytner, National Theatre

Coming soon

Stovepipe by Adam Brace
in collaboration with the National Theatre and The Bush Theatre

3 – 29 March 2009

For tickets: nationaltheatre.org/stovepipe

'One of the best promenade dramas I've seen.' Sir Tom Stoppard

HighTide Company

Artistic Directors	Samuel Hodges and Steven Jon Atkinson
Associate Producer	Henry Filloux-Bennett
Literary Associate	Mark Richards
Casting Associate	Charlotte Bevan
Voice Associate	John Tucker
Design Associates	takis (designer), Matt Prentice (lighting), Steve Mayo (sound)
Artistic Advisors	Jack Bradley, Robert Fox, Thelma Holt CBE, Tom Morris
President	Peter Fincham
Chairman	Mary Allen
Company Directors	Emily Blacksell, Sue Emmas, Rosie Hunter, Joyce Hytner OBE, Clare Parsons, Stephen Pidcock, Dallas Smith, Gaby Styles
Financial Advisor	James Midgley
Patrons	Sinéad Cusack, Sally Greene OBE, Sir David Hare, Bill Nighy

HighTide: A major initiative by the Old Possum's Practical Trust
Leading Corporate Sponsor: Lansons Communications

Resident company at Aldeburgh Music, Snape Maltings Concert Hall,
Snape, Suffolk, IP17 1SP

Contact: **HighTide, 24a St John Street, London WC2N 6AA**
Email: **info@hightidefestival.org** Telephone: **020 7566 9764**
Website: **www.hightidefestival.org**

bush theatre

'One of the most experienced prospectors of raw talent in Europe'
The Independent

The Bush Theatre is a world-famous home for new plays and an internationally renowned champion of playwrights. We discover, nurture and produce the best new playwrights from the widest range of backgrounds, and present their work to the highest possible standards. We look for exciting new voices that tell contemporary stories with wit, style and passion and we champion work that is both provocative and entertaining.

The Bush has produced hundreds of groundbreaking premieres since its inception 36 years ago. The theatre produces up to eight productions of new plays a year, many of them Bush commissions, and hosts guest productions by leading companies and artists from all over the world.

The Bush is widely acclaimed as the seedbed for the best new playwrights, many of whom have gone on to become established names in the entertainment industry, including Helen Blakeman, Amelia Bullmore, Richard Cameron, David Eldridge, Kevin Elyot, Jonathon Harvey, Dusty Hughes, Terry Johnson, Charlotte Jones, Dennis Kelly, Doug Lucie, Sharman Macdonald, Conor McPherson, Chloë Moss, Mark O'Rowe, Joe Penhall, Stephen Poliakoff, Philip Ridley, Billy Roche and Snoo Wilson. We also champion the introduction of new talent to the industry, whilst continuing to attract major acting and directing talents, including Frances Barber, Kate Beckinsale, Jim Broadbent, Simon Callow, Brian Cox, Lindsay Duncan, Joseph Fiennes, Mike Figgis, Patricia Hodge, Jane Horrocks, Bob Hoskins, Mike Leigh, Mike Newell, Stephen Rea, Alan Rickman, Tim Roth, Nadim Sawalha, Anthony Sher, John Simm, Alison Steadman, Julie Walters, Richard Wilson and Victoria Wood.

The Bush has won over one hundred awards, and developed an enviable reputation for touring its acclaimed productions nationally and internationally. Recent tours and transfers include the West End production of *Elling* (2007), the West End transfer and national tour of *Whipping It Up* (2007), a national tour of *Mammals* (2006), an international tour of *After the End* (2005-6), *adrenalin... heart* representing the UK in the Tokyo International Arts Festival (2004), the West End transfer (2002) and national tour of *The Glee Club* (2004), a European tour of *Stitching* (2003), and Off-Broadway transfers of *Howie the Rookie* and *Resident Alien*. Film adaptations include *Beautiful Thing* and *Disco Pigs*.

The Bush Theatre provides a free script-reading service, receiving over 1000 scripts through the post every year, and reading and responding to every one. This is one small part of a comprehensive playwrights' development programme which nurtures the relationship between writer and director, as well as playwright residencies and commissions. Everything that we do to develop playwrights focuses them towards a production on our stage or beyond. We have also launched an ambitious new education, training and professional development programme, **bush**futures, providing opportunities for different sectors of the community and professionals to access the expertise of Bush playwrights, directors, designers, technicians and actors, and to play an active role in influencing the future development of the theatre and its programme.

The Bush Theatre is extremely proud of its reputation for artistic excellence, its friendly atmosphere, and its undisputed role as a major force in shaping the future of British theatre.

Josie Rourke
Artistic Director

At The Bush Theatre

Artistic Director	**Josie Rourke**
General Manager	**Angela Bond**
Associate Director bushfutures	**Anthea Williams**
Associate Director	**James Grieve**
Finance Manager	**Viren Thakker**
Marketing Manager	**Alix Hearn**
Production Manager	**Sam Craven-Griffiths**
Assistant Producer	**Caroline Dyott**
Acting Development Manager	**Chantelle Staynings**
Artists' Administrator	**Tara Wilkinson**
Box Office Supervisor	**Clare Moss**
Box Office Assistants	**Natasha Bloor** **Kirsty Cox** **Ava Leman Morgan**
Front of House Duty Managers	**Kellie Batchelor** **Euan Forsyth** **Alex Hern** **Olly Lavery** **Ava Leman Morgan** **Glenn Mortimer** **Sam Plumb** **Rose Romain** **Lois Tucker**
Duty Technicians	**Deb Jones** **Sara Macleod** **George Maddocks** **Ben Sherratt** **Clare Spillman** **Shelley Stace** **Matthew Vile**
Associate Artists	**Tanya Burns** **Arthur Darvill** **Chloe Emmerson** **James Farncombe** **Richard Jordan** **Emma Laxton** **Paul Miller** **Lucy Osborne**
Associate Playwright	**Anthony Weigh**
Creative Associates	**Nathan Curry** **Charlotte Gwinner** **Clare Lizzimore** **George Perrin** **Hamish Pirie** **Dawn Walton**
Writer in Residence	**Jack Thorne**
Press Representative	**Ewan Thomson**
Resident Assistant Director	**Hannah Ashwell-Dickinson**
Intern	**Natasha Bloor**

The Bush Theatre
Shepherd's Bush Green
London W12 8QD

Box Office: 020 8743 5050
www.bushtheatre.co.uk

The Alternative Theatre Company Ltd. (The Bush Theatre)
is a Registered Charity number: 270080
Co. registration number 1221968 | VAT no. 228 3168 73

supported by

Be there at the beginning

Our work identifying and nurturing playwrights is only made possible through the generous support of our Patrons and other donors. Thank you to all those who have supported us during the last year.

If you are interested in finding out how to be involved, please visit the 'Support Us' section of www.bushtheatre.co.uk, or call 020 8743 3584.

bushfutures

bushfutures is a groundbreaking programme that allows our community and emerging practitioners and playwrights to access the expertise of Bush writers, directors, designers, technicians and actors.

We are devoted to finding and supporting The Bush artists of tomorrow.

bushfutures **Projects**

bushfutures creates exciting and innovative projects to engage emerging playwrights and produce their plays on The Bush stage. So far in 2008 projects have included **50 Ways to Leave Your Lover** and **The Halo Project. 50 Ways to Leave Your Lover** was written by five remarkable emerging playwrights and toured to Oxford, Norwich and the Latitude Festival before performing at The Bush Theatre. **The Halo Project** allowed Simon Vinnicombe to work with a large group of young people from Hammersmith and Fulham to develop a new play, **Turf**, which was performed by and for young people in our theatre.

bushfutures **in Schools**

bushfutures develops projects with schools, colleges and tertiary institutions. The Bush is one of Britain's leading New Writing companies. We share our talent and expertise with young people through tailor-made workshops which focus on playwriting, performance and the development of new work.

bushfutures **Associates**

Emerging practitioners make up a group of associates who are an integral part of The Bush community. They are invited to talks and workshops by leading theatre practitioners and involved in development events.

bushtalk

Throughout the year The Bush hosts discussions for the public between leading playwrights and theatre practitioners.

For more information contact **bushfutures@bushtheatre.co.uk**

I CAUGHT CRABS IN WALBERSWICK

Joel Horwood

For my best friends

I Caught Crabs in Walberswick was first presented as part of the HighTide Festival 2008 at The Cut, Halesworth, Suffolk on 2 May 2008, produced by Samuel Hodges and Steven Jon Atkinson, in a co-production with Eastern Angles. The cast was as follows:

FITZ	Joseph Arkley
WHEELER	David Hartley
DANI	Matti Houghton
ONE	Paul Trussell
TWO	Judith Scott

Director	Lucy Kerbel
Dramaturge	Beth Byrne for Neal Street Productions
Designer	takis
Lighting Designer	Matt Prentice
Sound Designer	Steve Mayo
Voice	John Tucker
Movement	Fernanda Prater for Punchdrunk

The production transferred to the Pleasance Courtyard, Edinburgh, on 1 August 2008, as part of the Edinburgh Festival Fringe, and then toured from 3 September to 11 October 2008. It transferred to The Bush Theatre, London, on 11 November 2008. The cast was as follows, with the following change to the original production team:

FITZ	Aaron Foy
WHEELER	Harry Hepple
DANI	Gemma Soul
ONE	Andrew Barron
TWO	Rosie Thomson

Movement	Shona Morris

Characters

WHEELER, *sixteen*
FITZ, *sixteen*
DANI, *sixteen*
ONE, *adult male*
TWO, *adult female*

ONE *and* TWO *double as all other characters:*

BOB, *Fitz's dad*
STEPH, *Wheeler's mum*
MAX, *Wheeler's dad*
URSULA, *Dani's mum*
JEREMY, *Dani's dad*
BOUNCER
COBB, *a policeman*

A dash (–) indicates an interruption or stopping short

An ellipsis (…) indicates a trailing off

All beats and pauses are to be adhered to at the discretion of the director and actors

Some words are written phonetically to convey the Suffolk dialect and accent

This text went to press before the end of rehearsals and so may differ slightly from the play as performed.

During the pre-set, ten filthy minutes of techno heaven. LOUD!!

ONE *and* TWO *acknowledge the presence of the audience with a look or a nod and then signal for the music to cut into the sounds of summer. They begin their presentation.*

FITZ *begins rolling a joint.*

TWO. Walberswick, a picturesque village on the east coast of England, also known as Hampstead-on-Sea.

ONE. This summer, expensive, family-friendly cars file along the A12 from as far away as Chalk Farm and Notting Hill to fill their usually empty second homes, dribble organic ice cream, and paddle in the beer-coloured sea.

TWO. Only nice people live in Walberswick.

ONE. Only the nicest.

WHEELER. We sign up for Psychology next year and we get crème bru-*laid*, café au-*laid* – Four girls to one.

FITZ. You gotta have Biology to do Psychology?

WHEELER. Like, 'C' or something.

FITZ. I should be revising.

WHEELER. Gonna be like a Lynx advert.

FITZ *lights the joint.*

ONE. This is Fitz and this is Wheeler.

WHEELER. How come you haven't squeezed that whitehead, get all the poison out?

FITZ (*covering it*). Make it worse.

WHEELER. Not with the double squeeze – Squeeze it 'til it bleeds, come here –

FITZ. What?

WHEELER. I'll do it – here.

A brief and silly struggle that almost jeopardises the joint before it stops.

TWO. On the hottest day of the hottest summer ever recorded, they've walked from the cheaper property in Reydon, to Walberswick's prime crab-fishing spot.

ONE (*indicating*). Rickety wooden bridge, muddy creek, crab-fishing.

TWO. It's four o'clock in the afternoon.

FITZ (*passing the joint*). That poem was in the English exam yesterdee, weren't it?

WHEELER. ...?

FITZ. He runs scissors through a Bunsen burner, passes 'em over, that one –

WHEELER. Armitage.

FITZ. You totally fell for that.

WHEELER. You branded me.

FITZ. S'only a scar, that'll fade, pansy.

ONE. We should clarify, these are those scrawny brown crabs you catch with bacon on a string, keep in a bucket for a bit, then chuck back.

WHEELER *takes a drag on the joint.*

WHEELER (*coughing*). Woah-woah-woah – What's all this? Weak as. (*Passing joint back.*) Barely affecting me.

FITZ. How come them kids already got a bucketful and you han't got no crabs?

WHEELER *looks at* FITZ.

WHEELER. How many people know about that?

FITZ. Not many.

ONE. Wheeler had slept with Tara Hodgkinson in a one-man pop-up tent on a school trip to Mid-Wales. Nicknames such as Crabby –

TWO. Hive-head.

6

ONE. Itchy.

TWO. Scratchy. Walker's Crab Bag.

ONE. The nicknames had stuck.

FITZ (*passing the joint*). Here y'are, Crabby-Claw, wash your hands first though, yeah?

WHEELER (*sarcastic*). That's so funny! D'you get that off *Two Pints of Lager and a Packet of Crisps*? (*Pulls on the joint.*) You know that French teacher? Does oral, pencil skirts, you know?

FITZ. Oral.

WHEELER (*passing the joint*). Yeah. It's on.

FITZ (*giggling*). Oral.

WHEELER. Exam today, she's s'posed ta go through the whole syllabus with everyone, right?

FITZ. Their oral exam.

WHEELER. Yeah – Shut up – She could go through anything from buying a croissant –

FITZ (*trying to pronounce it correctly*). Croissant.

WHEELER. – to what pets you've got. Know what she asks me? Asks me about my hobbies.

FITZ. Croissant.

WHEELER. *Mon passe temps*, yeah? She wants to know how I spend my personal time, I mean, it is on.

FITZ (*pulls on the joint*). Bite! You got a bite, look, two of 'em humping, pull 'em up!

WHEELER. Ugh –

FITZ. Pull 'em up, pull 'em up – Humping crabs, pull 'em up!

WHEELER. Stop saying 'Pull 'em up'.

FITZ. They love bacon like it's crack. You reckon they're gonna – like little tanks, raid the pig sties – 'Vee vant bacon! Vee vant zee bacon!' Quick, git 'em up, come on –

WHEELER. Crabs aren't German – (*Passes out.*)

FITZ. Wheels?

>FITZ *takes a long toke and looks around.*

>Shit.

>FITZ *holds* WHEELER*'s wrist for a pulse.*

TWO. For the past three years, Fitz has spent an hour before bed reading and re-reading the correct methods of resuscitation in the case of an emergency.

>FITZ *lets* WHEELER*'s hand fall.*

FITZ. Orlroit, not an emergency.

ONE. We'd like to present the one night that changes everything.

TWO. Before Wheeler pulled his whitey –

ONE. Sorry, his what?

TWO. Before Wheeler passed out, at two forty-five p.m., Fitz had just got in from a sweaty shift at the book-binding factory.

>*Sounds of an aeroplane computer game.*

BOB. It is FUCKEN HOT! (*Farts loudly.*)

TWO. When his mother died three years ago, Fitz's dad contracted 'The Condition'. Instead of working he plays aeroplane-simulation games, not the fun fighter games with Spitfires and stuff, the games that involve hours of flying in straight lines.

FITZ. I'm goin' down Budgens, gettin' lunch… Got paid, could get steak, veg, make some roasties… Get a Sara Lee Double Chocolate Gateau –

BOB. Huh?

FITZ. Sara Lee Double –

BOB. You want me to crash and kill four hundred innocent passengers? Trying to fly these people from Mon-fucken-golia and you're talking 'bout – what you talking 'bout? LUNCH! Talkin' 'bout lunch –

FITZ. I'm just gonna go down –

BOB. Budgens, whoopdee fucken – hang on – (*In a special pilot voice.*) Hamburg, come in Hamburg, this is Flight 17-24, requesting clearance for transit through your airspace, over.

FITZ. If I 'on't ask, you won't eat proper.

BOB (*to* FITZ). Nearly made me forget ta ask for clearance, banging on about GSOHs and exams...

FITZ. GCSEs.

BOB. Already got a job, and your football, you're a natural, like your old man. (*Into computer.*) Thank you, Hamburg.

FITZ. Might get a bit for the freezer. It's pretty easy if you wanna cook it –

BOB. Hang on. (*Pauses game.*) What's that mean?

FITZ. Might not be in every night, you know? I'm still pickin' your shifts up –

BOB. That's reduced hours, in't it? Coupla shifts a week?

FITZ. But these exams, revising – It's knackering, Dad.

BOB. Well, sorry but I in't in no state, am I? You in't gonna leave me to it, are ya? What if I gotta go out – Everyone staring, asking stuff, knowing, and I get – My breath – I'm – (*Farts.*) It's a condition.

FITZ. I'm just sayin' suffin' might come up with football or with my friends –

BOB. You can do that, course you can, in't a baby, dun't need constant – (*Farts.*) That better be sweat.

FITZ. I'm goin' a Budgens.

BOB. Oi – (*In pilot voice.*) Get some Sara Lee Double Chocolate Gateau! Over.

TWO. Wheeler's mother is a driving instructress.

ONE. He's never really been certain what his father does for a living, he just knows that his dad occasionally gets nice new work cars.

TWO. At about three p.m. Wheeler is on the internet researching mysterious disappearances and trying to get more friends than Fitz on social-networking sites.

STEPH. We'll get you driving round the industrial estate tomorrow, keep your practice up.

MAX. It's no use, he's on MyFace.

WHEELER. Er, Facebook, Dad.

STEPH. He doesn't have to revise all the time, Max.

MAX. I know that, *Steph*.

STEPH. In fact, Scott, your predicted results, with all the work you did on your coursework, you're doing great. I mean, we're not going to get overexcited but they open up some doors, don't they?

WHEELER. Mmm.

WHEELER *gets a text.*

TWO. Wheeler's texting Chloë, his long-term girlfriend.

MAX *and* STEPH *watch as* WHEELER *formulates his text.*

MAX. How much money do you two spend texting each other?

WHEELER. Dad.

STEPH. You two are just like we were.

WHEELER. Ugh.

STEPH. Well, we can drop you at Gemma's barbecue, if you want. Or there's a Hawaiian in the freezer.

MAX. Better let him out! (*Mimes being stuck.*) Freezer.

STEPH. It's our twentieth anniversary so we're going for Chinese, might not be back 'til late.

MAX. We did reserve a table, didn't we?

WHEELER*'s phone rings, he shoos the parents away.*

STEPH. You said you were going to.

MAX. I distinctly remember –

STEPH. Max! Now we're not going to eat until God knows when.

WHEELER (*answering phone*). Wass-zizurp home-piece?

FITZ. What's going on? What happened at the party?

WHEELER. You were a little bitch and pussied out, is what happened.

FITZ. Was Tina there?

WHEELER. Oh my – You know we studied the suction power of limpets? Nothing compared to Tina Everton. She has opened up my world sexually, the bar has been raised, my friend.

FITZ. What about Chloë?

WHEELER. This is strictly need-to-know, alright, gangster? Where're you?

FITZ. Budgens, getting food, revising.

WHEELER. When are you gonna stop being such a gayboy and come out? Walberswick's crawling with posh girls.

FITZ. On a Thursdee?

WHEELER. On a hot-as-hell Thursday of exam leave, course it is! Fo' sho! Come on, Goose, Maverick needs a wingman.

FITZ. What does that even mean?

WHEELER. Bring some gear, I lost that one you rolled for me.

FITZ. What!?

WHEELER. Cleaner did my room. Gone. Are you coming out or are you gonna try to buy yourself a life in Budgens?

FITZ. Don't you have an exam tomorrow?

WHEELER. We both have, knob-jockey, Biology.

FITZ. Shit.

WHEELER. You're a first-aid genius, Fitz, you should be writing that exam, now grow a set and let's get –

MAX. Not going out, are you, Scott?

WHEELER. Er – Ten minutes. (*Hangs up.*) Just collecting seaweed samples from the beach.

MAX. It's not a big deal, I'm just, er… I took my laptop into repairs. My work laptop. Do you know what I'm driving at?

WHEELER. …

MAX. I know, sometimes, when you're young – hell, sometimes when your mother's away, even I do it. Reduces stress, raises the function of the immune system… Do you know what…? All I'm saying, Scott, is that it's a natural thing to do. It's completely natural to have a tommy tank.

WHEELER. A what?

MAX. I don't want to beat around the bush… They made the repairs and found some mpegs… Just don't use my computer to look at those, okay? I mean, they asked me questions about my marriage –

WHEELER. Oh God.

MAX. What's wrong with your own computer? Now I have to buy the bloody thing, I'm not – It's not an unnatural – I mean, it is a natural thing, just not with my…

WHEELER. Yeah, sorry, I'm sorry –

MAX. She was limber, though. Bendy. Almost Olympic standard –

WHEELER. Bye, Dad.

TWO. A kind of dread begins to fill Max as he realises that he never found his own father as ridiculous as he feels now.

Beat.

ONE. When he leaves, Wheeler takes the set of keys with a door key, car key and a bottle opener disguised as a key.

TWO. By the end of this presentation, he will have used both the keys and the rusting Swiss Army knife that clatter in his pocket.

FITZ. That was the biggest whitey, looked like Casper the Friendly Ghost.

TWO. So, Wheeler and Fitz are here at a little after four o'clock.

ONE. On the little bridge, over the creek, in Walberswick. Crabs escaping their forgotten bucket and bedding down in the mud.

FITZ. I gotta go.

WHEELER (*giving* FITZ *the pistol fingers*). Gemma's thing tonight.

FITZ. I only revised evolution, barely know about these crabs never mind naked apes or whatever –

WHEELER. What about Miriam Saunders?

FITZ. It's my last chance for sixth form, I can't –

WHEELER *nipple-cripples* FITZ.

WHEELER. Miriam 'The Arse' Saunders – One arse-presso to go, please, ma'am!

FITZ. Why do all your sex words involve coffee?

DANI *enters. 'Bend Over Beethoven' by !!! begins.*

TWO. This is Daniella Hurling-Challice.

ONE. No one at Daniella's –

DANI. It's Dani.

ONE. Right. No one at Dani's school remembers who they heard it from first, but everyone's sure that Dani's father died whilst researching global warming in the Antarctic.

TWO. Dani's father isn't. Actually. Dead. He's a best-selling popular psychologist. In order to feel closer to him, Dani religiously fills in the *Psychologies Magazine* quiz. Today's title is 'Are You a Self-Saboteur?'

ONE. Yes, she goes to an all-girls school, but Dani knows boys. Dani knows lots of boys.

DANI *cues 'House of Cards' by Radiohead.*

She sits behind the boys, facing away from them on the bridge.

DANI. Excuse me? I can't quite reach… I don't suppose you boys could rub a little of this into my back? Unless it makes you uncomfortable or something?

The boys take the suntan lotion.

TWO. Dani's mother, Ursula, moved to Walberswick for the light, Constable and 'to get away from it all'.

ONE. Dani had left the house a couple of hours earlier, after –

URSULA. You do more of those silly magazine quizzes than you do prep.

DANI. What makes you think I need prep?

URSULA. Well, you sleep most of the day, sunbathe when awake and generally mope about the house.

DANI. Mope.

URSULA. You used to be so bright and energetic –

DANI. Things used to be different, Ursula.

URSULA. Are you going to turn that music down?

Amused, DANI *stops the music.*

Thank you. Of course you can read your magazines, I didn't come in here to talk about that. I came in because I wanted – Well, I've been meaning to ask you if you still pray?

DANI. Why don't you do anything except ask me questions?

URSULA. I do things, I do do things, I paint every day, I'm in the studio every day –

DANI. But it's all in what you don't do, isn't it, Ursula?

URSULA. It's the manipulation of negative space, of course it's in what I don't do, it's art.

DANI. Isn't art a fashionable name for moping?

URSULA. I'm only asking if you still believe in prayer, no need to bite my head off –

DANI. Doesn't it say 'Chapel' on the school invoices?

URSULA. You used to pray. With Granny, with me –

DANI. For toys.

URSULA. I want you to come with me this Sunday, Daniella, for some quiet time together –

DANI. It's Dani.

URSULA. I want you to come to church with me, 'Dani'.

DANI. This is new, wasn't it dreamcatchers and crystals last week? Did I miss an article in *Tatler*?

URSULA. Why do you call me Ursula?

DANI. Is church suddenly the 'in' thing? The new boho-chic?

URSULA. Why do you call me Ursula?

DANI. Did you know your name means 'bear' in Latin?

URSULA. This is too difficult.

DANI. Then give up.

URSULA. I don't want to shout at you.

DANI. Why not!?

URSULA. These exams will help you to get where you want to be in life –

DANI. Was it passing your exams or divorcing a millionaire that got you here?

URSULA *slaps* DANI.

ONE. Ursula didn't expect the lingering burn in her hand. She had never hit anyone before.

URSULA. I'm going to go for a walk.

URSULA *exits.*

'House of Cards' by Radiohead kicks in, and the boys are still rubbing DANI*'s back.*

ONE. For the boys, Dani is like lighter fuel on a barbecue. Wheeler can't believe it.

WHEELER. I can't believe it. I'm rubbing a ten.

TWO. He considers his first moves.

WHEELER. Yeah, baby, what's happening? Wheeler.

ONE. Would've been a confident start.

WHEELER. Sorry, I think you need a little more sunblock, maybe loo-wer down…

TWO. Sex pest.

WHEELER. You got a boyfriend?

TWO. Too direct.

FITZ. I'm Fitz.

Music cuts out.

WHEELER (*quiet*). You bastard.

FITZ. This here's Wheeler, some people call him Crabby, he had to shave his head cos Tara Hodgkinson –

WHEELER. No one calls me Crabby.

FITZ (*offering the joint*). You're from London, right?

WHEELER. That stuff can be pretty harsh, so –

DANI. How could you tell I'm from London? (*Taking a drag*.)

FITZ (*shrugs*). You're on this beach.

WHEELER. And girls round here are a bit Jordan, but you're totally, like – (*Masculine sound of approval*.)

FITZ. You got a house here then?

DANI. My mum has.

FITZ. Exam leave, is ut?

DANI *smokes – nods*.

That sucks.

WHEELER. Us too. Exam leave, I mean, not suck – we don't suck. We're really fun.

FITZ. Where do you go to school, then?

DANI. Boarding school, middle of nowhere, with the little skirts, long socks, you know, ridiculous.

WHEELER. You got – You got an exam tomorrow?

DANI. Nah, next one's Astronomy.

FITZ. What?

DANI. I know. It's an extra one, I only took it cos Dad wanted me to – Look, I could do with an actual night out, you don't know anywhere – ?

WHEELER. Well, there's this barbecue thing tonight.

FITZ. Or we could get booze by tomorrow night, if you're about then –

DANI (*stretching*). Sneaking booze behind bushes is, like, bum-out. I wanna dance, go wild where people can see me, you know?

WHEELER. There's a club. In Lowestoft, there's a… Could try to get a train or – right, Fitz?

DANI. A club?

WHEELER. Totally, Beccles train leaves around eight, or something, eight-oh-six –

FITZ. What, Bluenotes?

WHEELER. Bluenotes, yeah, we go there loads. Like, loads. All the time.

FITZ. Yeah.

DANI (*to* FITZ). We barely know each other.

FITZ. Git to know each other tonight, I 'on't mean – I in't being a perv or nothin' –

DANI. You're sure we can get in? We're not gonna end up stuck on another beach?

WHEELER. Nah, yeah, fine, we'll get in, yeah.

DANI*'s phone starts ringing.*

DANI. Okay, eight, Beccles?

WHEELER. Done and done.

DANI. I've gotta… [answer this.]

WHEELER. Oh, yeah, right.

FITZ. See ya there.

WHEELER. Yeah, yeah – maybe you will.

> FITZ *scowls at* WHEELER.

> DANI *answers the phone*.

DANI. Dad!

> JEREMY *is trying to hear over kiddie madness*.

JEREMY. Darling, I have got to be quick.

DANI. That's fine, it's just –

JEREMY. If it's about your mother, she has deep-seated emotional issues, try to get on with your work –

DANI. I know but –

JEREMY. Can't talk now, going away with Maggie and the kids tonight, really long drive from up here.

DANI. Where to? Blakeney?

JEREMY (*to the kids*). Boys, I don't think anyone appreciates violence – Stop! Dani, help me out, you're a grown up now, aren't you?

DANI. Yeah, I just – I don't like it here.

JEREMY. You must know people there.

DANI. No.

JEREMY. Well, you can't stay in London alone.

DANI. How long are you gonna be in Blakeney?

JEREMY. We're aiming to be there by eight in the morning –

DANI. No, I mean, maybe I could stay with you or –

JEREMY. Darling, I'm sorry but it's a crucial period in the boys' development of self, they need a nuclear family with clear boundaries – Shouldn't you be revising anyway?

DANI. I am.

JEREMY. Your predicted results are promising, I forwarded them to my old fellow at St John's College, so glad you took Astronomy, anyway he wants to hear how you get on as soon as possible.

DANI. St John's?

JEREMY. Never say 'St John's' without saying 'College', darling.

DANI. Sorry.

JEREMY. Of course, you can't just be 'promising', at some point you'll have to actually achieve something, but they're the best college at Cambridge, barely look at more than five girls a year – (*To the kids*.) Crispin.

DANI. Dad, I don't know if I'm –

JEREMY. CRISPIN! (*To* DANI.) I've really got to go, the boys are rejecting some ground rules.

DANI. But about Cambridge –

JEREMY. Okay, bye, love, bye!

'Sheila' by Jamie T underscores FITZ *and* WHEELER *getting ready.*

ONE. The boys had only heard of Bluenotes because Darren Midmore once managed to get in and get off with a thirty-two-year-old mother of two.

WHEELER. Lucky bastard, but we're going with a ten.

FITZ. She's definitely a ten.

WHEELER. You were the rizzle dizzle, man. (*Sean Connery impression*.) 'Hello, would you care to join us for a night at Bluenotes?'

FITZ (*Sean Connery impression*). 'Miss Moneypenny, would you like to accompany us on a short train voyage?'

WHEELER. Worth skipping Gemma's on the off-chance she has to bend down to pick something up.

FITZ. I should be revising.

WHEELER. Cramming before an exam makes you crap. Fact. Exam's not 'til ten, I'll give you a hand in the morning –

FITZ. I'm working six 'til half nine, I'm – (*Shakes his head.*)

WHEELER. Pull a sicky.

FITZ. Dad'd lose the job.

WHEELER. It's not his job to lose no more, is it? Got your own life. It's not like GCSEs mean anything, anyway.

FITZ. Not if you stay on, they dun't.

WHEELER. This girl was totally flirting with you – She's not even a girl, she's, like... ARGH!

FITZ. Reckon she's gonna show up?

WHEELER. She picked you out of everyone on the beach.

FITZ. Us.

WHEELER. You. Suck it up. Now, do I look gay or super-pimp? Be honest.

Music cuts out.

STEPH. Here's your month's allowance, we booked you a cab for ten o'clock.

ONE. Max and Steph drop the boys outside Gemma's house on their way to The Golden Panda.

STEPH. Tell Chloë we said hello.

MAX. Don't do anything twattish.

TWO. As soon as Wheeler's parents were out of sight, the boys turned their backs on the burned burgers and walked down to the station.

ONE. At Beccles train station there's a wall covered in engraved graffiti.

FITZ (*looking at the wall*). 1996.

ONE. The names and dates of relationships, the gravestones of friendships.

FITZ. 1990.

ONE. Every letter, penknife deep, in the blood-red brick.

WHEELER. Next year we'll be heading up Lowestoft all the time. Pass my test, pick you up, go and get crunkin', drink sizzurp, get *lizz-aid...*

FITZ. '88...

WHEELER. Keep playing for Lowestoft, might get scouted, go London, Essex, more girls in Essex. You'd be outta here, escape velocity, gone, *hasta luego, cabrones.*

FITZ. 1979.

WHEELER (*referring to the wall*). How many of those you think stuck around? None of 'em. London's the other end of these tracks, hop on and – (*Makes a sound like a rocket heading for the moon.*)

TWO. Fitz noticed two names he recognised. The names of his parents, either side of a number four.

WHEELER. Hah! 'Wang' – There's actually someone called Wang up there! Hey, I got a knife.

FITZ. What you gonna do with it, Ray Mears? Make fire?

DANI *enters.* WHEELER *doesn't notice.*

WHEELER. Get our names up on the wall of fame, and maybe, like, 'Wheeler 4 Chloë' or 'Fitz and Wheels' –

FITZ. Orlroit?

DANI. Fitz, yeah? What's that short for...?

FITZ. Carl Stracchan.

WHEELER. Wheeler's my surname, so...

DANI. I'm Dani.

FITZ. You look... You look really good.

DANI (*giggles*). All my good clothes are still at school –

FITZ. Nah, looks good.

DANI. Thank you.

WHEELER. Let's get *twisted*!

> WHEELER *passes* DANI *the bottle*. DANI *drinks*.

FITZ. You're gonna love this place.

WHEELER. Train's coming any minute.

DANI (*reacting to the drink*). Ergh – What is that?

WHEELER. Liz-nambrini, baby! (*Swigs*.)

DANI. What's that mean?

FITZ. Lambrini.

WHEELER. We're gonna get down like it's Meh-hee-ho [Mexico] Town!

DANI. I just came back from there.

WHEELER. No way! The beaches out there are like –

DANI. Ohmygod, did you go to the Pacific? The beach from that film?

WHEELER. Say-wa-ten-ayo? [*Zihuatanejo*.] Yeah.

ONE. The conversation on the train is filled with places Fitz only knows from the postcards Wheeler sends.

Distant club music builds slowly.

TWO. The bright lights of Lowestoft!

ONE. Famous as the place where Joseph Conrad attempted suicide.

TWO. The bottle lasts almost the whole wobbly walk from station to club.

WHEELER (*finishing the bottle and almost puking*). That stuff is dope!

ONE. The bump and roll of basslines drifts out to sea from Bluenotes.

DANI. Come on, I'm bursting!

WHEELER. Piss fear.

FITZ. He's like this in the showers after PE too. Dunno how he does it.

DANI. Does what?

FITZ. Gits a lot o' girls, dun't he?

WHEELER. I'm not that far away.

FITZ. Y'orlroit?

DANI (*giggling*). Bit drunk. Need a wee.

FITZ. That's just up here.

> DANI *holds* FITZ's *hand, squats, and wees.*

ONE. As Dani steadies herself and lets a rivulet of piss –

TWO. What he means is that Fitz has never experienced anything normal about girls, he's kissed them, had the odd wet cuddle with them but in terms of something real…

FITZ. I thought when they wee'd, fairies took it all away.

TWO. Fitz has never held a girl's hand before, in fact, the last woman he hugged was his mother.

DANI. Thanks.

> DANI *kisses* FITZ's *cheek.*

WHEELER. Jesus, I think I just broke the hosepipe ban, I was slashing like a racehorse.

ONE. The queue to the club! When you're sixteen and look it, it's best to position yourself in front of some girls. Normally, the bouncer will wave you through to get a look.

WHEELER. I'm so hot I can't tell if I've pissed myself. Is there a mark?

FITZ. Nah.

WHEELER. We don't look old enough. He's gonna ask for ID cos we don't look old enough.

FITZ. Relax.

WHEELER. My ID says I'm a twenty-eight-year-old doctor, Fitz. We're not getting in, we need a Plan B.

FITZ. Stop being such a vaginal openin', we'll get in.

WHEELER. Is she pissing again?

FITZ. Talking to a fella.

WHEELER. You let her talk to someone else? She likes you, mate, I mean it.

FITZ. Let's just get in the club.

WHEELER. What are you, all meat and no veg? I'm telling you, man, girls cream 'emselves round you, gonna be feeding the horse tonight! (*Rubs fingers together and makes a squeaking sound.*)

Music leaps in clarity and volume as if a door is briefly opened. They shuffle closer to the BOUNCER.

Just, if he doesn't let us in, what are we gonna do?

FITZ. God's sake.

WHEELER. We finished the bottle, din't we?

FITZ. Dun't worry about it.

WHEELER. There's nothing to drink –

FITZ. You worrying?

WHEELER. I'm not worrying.

FITZ. You're worrying.

WHEELER. You're corrupting a posh girl. You can get fox-hunted for that these days, you should be worrying.

Music leaps in clarity and volume as if a door is briefly opened. They shuffle closer to the BOUNCER.

BOUNCER. Wait there, son.

WHEELER (*to* FITZ). He just called me 'son', d'you hear that?

FITZ. Dun't worry 'bout it, bouncers are twats, it's how they talk.

Enter DANI.

DANI. Miss me?

WHEELER. You've been missing out on fun time over here, where'd you go?

DANI (*to* FITZ). What's up with Dad?

FITZ. His old man found all his porn.

WHEELER. Why would you tell her that?

FITZ. Why you using your dad's work computer anyway, got your own.

DANI (*giggling*). Oh no.

WHEELER. Faster, for the films and...

DANI. What kind of films?

WHEELER. Just natural films.

BOUNCER. In you come, lads.

21:30 – Chinese-restaurant music.

TWO. Max and Steph have finally got a table at The Golden Panda.

ONE. Steph orders her usual.

STEPH. Sweet-and-sour chicken with egg-fried rice and can we get some prawn crackers while we wait? Thank you.

MAX. Yeah... Er...

TWO. Something inside Max snaps.

MAX. The king-du with mandarina pork and kung-po duck with hoisin, please.

STEPH. Max? We don't have any Pepto-Bismol.

MAX. I just want to eat something I can barely pronounce for a change. Thank you. Thanks.

DANI. Two Carling and a WKD.

22:00 – 'Let There Be Light' by Justice kicks in.

TWO. This is the kind of club where the walls sweat.

DANI. If I wanted two boys at one time I'd get two boys at one time.

FITZ. No way!

WHEELER. Why're you so sure?

DANI. Cos I'm a girl.

FITZ. She's roit.

WHEELER. Mental, in't she?

DANI. Boys are all slags, and everyone wants to try a three-some –

FITZ. With two girls, yeah.

WHEELER. Slags!? We're players!

FITZ. Two girls one boy, that's…

DANI. Players!

WHEELER. Fo' she-zee.

FITZ. Dun't lump me in with him.

DANI. Players? You don't know what a girl wants – (*Pinching* WHEELER*'s cheek.*) You're cute widdle boys.

WHEELER. I know what a girl wants.

FITZ. He dun't.

WHEELER. I'm a man – we're men.

FITZ. He in't.

WHEELER (*re:* DANI*'s drink*). What is that?

DANI. Horrible, gotta get some sugar before we hit the shots.

Music cuts into 'Wish You Were Here' by Pink Floyd.

ONE. After a four-hour walk and a heated conversation with Dani's father about Daniella and behavioural theory, Ursula has finished her second bottle of wine.

URSULA (*looking at a packet*). Pro Plus…

ONE. She's found her daughter's revision drugs.

URSULA (*looking at another packet*). Ritalin… (*Takes one*.)

ONE. And soon she will ensure that Dani's magazines are at right angles to the surfaces and that the kitchen herbs are in alphabetical order from left to right.

22:15 – The middle of 'Drop the Pressure' by Mylo.

WHEELER. Yeah, the DJ, yeah, I mean, I don't *know* him know him, he just went to my school, you know –

DANI. With you and Fitz.

WHEELER. Me and Fitz, yeah, but people know Fitz cos of his football, he's, like –

DANI. Isn't your girlfriend gonna be jealous?

WHEELER. …

DANI. You coming out with me like this, isn't she gonna be jealous? You've got a girlfriend, right?

WHEELER. Hah!

DANI. What's her name?

WHEELER. What?

DANI. Can't remember?

WHEELER. Where's Fitz?

DANI. Getting the drinks. What's her name?

WHEELER. Chloë. Her name's Chloë.

Beat.

DANI. I'm gonna get some water.

DANI *leaves*.

22:30 – a violent vinyl scratch to 'Hustler' by Simian Mobile Disco.

WHEELER. Fancies you, Fitzo!

FITZ. Nah.

> WHEELER *makes the international hand gesture for sex.*

> What time is it?

WHEELER. Who cares?

FITZ. This is mental, what'm I doin'?

WHEELER. You can revise before your shift, all-nighter, couple of Red Bulls, you'll nail it.

FITZ. That bouncer keeps lookin' at us.

WHEELER. Whatever, don't worry about it.

FITZ. She say she fancied me? Cos I got that, you know –

WHEELER. That vibe? Course you got that vibe, she practices kissing with other girls, starved of men, then this big football-playing – She's like your Lady Chatterley!

> *23:00 – 'D.A.N.C.E.' by Justice.* DANI *dances over to* FITZ.

FITZ. I dun't dance.

DANI. Neither do I, just wobble a bit.

FITZ. You wobble very nicely.

DANI. I bet you do too. Come on. Dance like your mum at weddings or whatever.

> *Beat.*

FITZ. Do you want another drink?

DANI. Are you trying to get me drunk?

FITZ. No.

DANI. You're trying to get me drunk.

FITZ. Nah.

DANI. Wheeler's got a girlfriend.

> *Beat.*

(*Touching* FITZ's *face*.) How'd you get that? He said you were a bruiser. You two go back a long way?

FITZ. Best mate.

DANI. Suit each other.

FITZ. What?

DANI. I said that you suit each other.

Beat.

It's so hot in here!

DANI *takes something off.*

BOB. Fucken boy, fucken fuck off without a fucken square meal for his fucken dad fuck.

TWO. Driven by hunger, Bob has found the freezer.

BOB. The hell said fish had fucken fingers anyway, they han't even got hands, think fish can fucken text? (*Farts loudly.*) They can't even oopen doors, even velociraptors can oopen fucken doors.

23:30 – the club music kicks in but in that echoey distant way that you get in toilets.

WHEELER. Why not the boys' toilets?

DANI (*giggling*). Cubicles.

WHEELER. That bouncer saw us come in.

DANI *gets the giggles. Bumping into the boys as she searches her belongings for a wrap.*

DANI. Shh.

WHEELER. What you doing?

FITZ (*to* WHEELER). Shut up.

DANI (*giggling*). …Giggles…

WHEELER. You're smashed.

DANI *removes a plastic wrap from her knickers, still giggling.*

DANI. Hiding – Hiding always makes me laugh, it's a self-sabotage thing –

Violent knocks on the door.

BOUNCER. One at a time!

DANI. Lick your fingers.

WHEELER. What?

DANI. Lick your fingers.

FITZ *tentatively puts his finger in his mouth.*

DANI *takes* WHEELER*'s finger in her mouth.*

Violent knocks on the door.

BOUNCER. Come on.

DANI (*to the boys*). Dab.

They all dab their fingers into the tiny plastic bag in DANI*'s palm.*

DANI *puts her finger in* FITZ*'s mouth.* WHEELER *puts his finger in* DANI*'s mouth.*

WHEELER. Well, dun't leave me out –

DANI *puts* FITZ*'s finger in* WHEELER*'s mouth.*

BOYS. Ergh!

WHEELER *is disgusted by the taste.*

BOUNCER. OUT OF THAT TOILET NOW!

FITZ. What happens next?

WHEELER. It's not affecting me.

TWO. It's almost midnight in The Golden Panda.

MAX (*a little drunk*). Let's not go yet, they don't close for another hour! We're both pissed, we can't drive. Come on.

STEPH. I'm not drunk.

MAX. Waiter!? More of that rice stuff… Booze! Here. Please.

STEPH. We both have to work in the morning.

MAX (*to another table*). Sorry, didn't mean to shout. (*To STEPH.*) I'm gonna call in sick tomorrow.

STEPH. I told you, you should have ordered your usual.

MAX. I'm not really sick – Just – Let's not stick to the schedule. For once, let's not behave like…

STEPH. You've been weird all evening, Max, is something up?

MAX. Nothing's up.

STEPH. Is something up?

MAX. No.

STEPH. Something's up, isn't it?

MAX. So what if he fancies a little tug every now and then he's a teenager –

STEPH. I knew something was up –

MAX. How did we get so old and so fucking boring?!

Beat.

STEPH *downs her sake.*

00:00 – the music kicks in, ear-splittingly loud – 'New Jack' by Justice.

WHEELER. YEEEAH!!

FITZ. FUCKEN TUNE!! I love you, Wheeler!!

WHEELER (*to FITZ*). Your eyes are massive! Woah-woah-woah-woah – Let me see your eyes, let me see your eyes, your eyes are massive too – What are mine like, are my eyes massive?

FITZ. YEAH!

DANI, WHEELER *and* FITZ *are going wild as* ONE *commentates.*

ONE. Fitz is doing what is commonly called the 'Freak Out', over there. Wheeler's combining the 'Salute to the Bass' with the 'Serve and Volley', I believe. And Dani… What is that? 'Walk Like a King'? I think that's 'Walk Like a King'.

WHEELER. Why haven't we always done this?

FITZ. Water? Water? I'm gonna get some water. Want water, yeah? Want water?

FITZ *leaves*.

DANI. I'm so glad I met you!

WHEELER. Seriously, you're so cool!

DANI. I need people like you!

WHEELER. Dani-Dani-Dani!

DANI. Cos you know you know you know that film that film *The Attack of the Fifty-Foot Woman* I love that film that's how it feels like you're so fucking big really really big and you wanna smash everything up but really like stamp on barns and pick people up and they're screaming ahh I feel that big but only inside I feel that big inside you know I used to come on holiday round here me my mum my dad and but we'd go to the beach and build castles and stomp on 'em and it was better when you built a really big one really all with and but you stomp it cos you know it feels really but you're just you're a tiny person just tiny –

Music cuts out.

WHEELER. I think this stuff might be having a bit of an effect now.

Music kicks back in.

DANI. What?

WHEELER. Yeah!

DANI. You gonna help me get somewhere?

WHEELER. You're so unbelievably fucken cool! Cos normally hot girls are like 'Oh I'm me' or whatever –

DANI. WHEELER! Tonight, later, I need to get somewhere, you gonna help me?

WHEELER. Course! What is it, house party?

DANI. Yeah, house party, yeah. Come here.

WHEELER. What?

Beat.

DANI. Who you looking for? Come here.

DANI *kisses* WHEELER.

WHEELER *kisses* DANI *back.*

FITZ *witnesses* WHEELER *and* DANI *snogging.*

ONE. Watching them kiss, Fitz can't understand what he's feeling. The only thing he can equate it to is coming home early one day to find his mum's medication scattered on the flowerbeds.

FITZ *drinks. Attempts to dance but the fun has gone.*

Fitz decides to be calm, not to react as he normally would and –

FITZ *punches* ONE. *Music cuts out.*

TWO. Two bouncers and a set of stairs later, the boys are securely on their first ever comedown.

DANI. Does it hurt?

FITZ. I dunno – I just –

DANI. We really got kicked out.

TWO. It's almost one o'clock in the morning, they're sat on the warm kerb.

WHEELER *spots something and begins looking around, mildly panicked.*

DANI (*trying to hold it*). How's your hand?

FITZ. Fine.

TWO. Wheeler sees that they're not far from The Golden Panda.

DANI. Wheeler?

WHEELER. Huh? Yeah, fine.

TWO. He can feel the conversation about how to get home closing in on them, he can feel tomorrow coming, then results day, the decisions –

ONE. He crosses to a silver Ford Focus parked opposite.

DANI. I think it was right, you did the right thing.

ONE. The smooth-action driver's door opens easily.

FITZ. I in't a violent fella, I'm just –

DANI. Protective.

FITZ. Protecting, yeah – You have a good night before then?

DANI. Yeah.

FITZ. Good, weren't it?

DANI. Wheeler, what are you doing?

WHEELER. Just keep an eye out, alright?

FITZ. We've only ever hotwired a lawnmower –

DANI. Are you helping me?

WHEELER. I said I would.

FITZ. Leave it, Wheeler, she's impressed, alright?

DANI. Someone's coming.

ONE. She's right, someone's coming.

FITZ. I've been paid, I'll get us a cab, let's go!

TWO. The club's kicking out, people are coming.

WHEELER. Don't need a cab.

    DANI *squeals with excitement and piles in.*

FITZ. Wheeler, it's a car, it's serious, we go now and –

    The engine revs hard.

DANI. Ohmygod.

WHEELER (*to* DANI). Music's there.

DANI. Ohmygod!

FITZ. Get out now, no one'd say nothing.

TWO. Somebody shouts, maybe at them.

WHEELER. Fitz?

ONE. People are close now.

> DANI *turns on the music: 'The Girls' by Calvin Harris kicks in.*

> FITZ *crams into the backseat as the car revs, stalls…*

TWO. The Ford Focus revs, stalls then tears along the seafront at twenty-five miles an hour in second gear.

FITZ. Woah – Left side, left.

Music kicks back in.

DANI. Follow signs for Great Yarmouth.

ONE. Wheeler's feeding the road through his hands, out of suburbia down the B-roads.

TWO. Passing fens and caravan parks, heading north.

FITZ. This in't fightin' bouncers or smokin' biftas, it's jail or – or –

WHEELER. Paranoid!

FITZ. Fucken jail.

DANI. He's a good driver – You're a good driver.

WHEELER. Mirroring, signalling, manoeuvring-ing

The music cuts into a bleeping smoke alarm.

TWO. The smoke alarm in Bob's house has relentlessly marked each second for the past half an hour.

BOB. I can be louder 'n you can! BEEP-fucken-BEEP!

TWO. After the microwave out-foxed him, and the gas oven took most of his eyebrows, Bob tried calling for a take-away. Every time he was asked what he wanted, his words stuck in his throat and he would hang up in a panic. Finally he had resolved that the frozen fish fingers would cook best in the toaster.

BOB *tries to eat but involuntarily coughs a mouthful out. The alarm continues to sound.*

Beat. BOB *takes in what's happening around him.*

BOB. Hell am I doin'?

TWO. In the next few minutes, Bob will decide to smash the smoke alarm to pieces and have to restore calm in the house by flying from Johannesburg to Norwich Airport.

Music kicks back in. FITZ, DANI *and* WHEELER *are still driving.*

FITZ. Eyes on the road, *Grand Theft Auto.*

DANI. There must be somewhere we can get some Smizz-ernoff.

FITZ. Where we even gooin'?

WHEELER. She said up here.

FITZ. How far?

DANI. Ugh. Fitz!

FITZ. You're hammered, directin' us somewhere we han't never heard of.

DANI. Hammered?

WHEELER (*turning to* FITZ). Fitz, don't worry about it.

FITZ. Watch the road.

WHEELER. What's happened to Fitz? What have you done with my friend!

DANI. Fuck!

A screech of brakes and a palpable thud.

TWO. Steph has paid for the cab home and –

STEPH *saves* MAX *from falling.*

STEPH. Wa-hey! (*Holding* MAX *up*.) Keys are here, some-where. Shall we sit?

MAX. Not sit.

MAX *sits*.

Why did you sleep with Derek?

STEPH. Derek?

MAX (*nods*). In high school.

STEPH. Derek Pieterson?

MAX. You're the only person I've slept with. Only ever – There's no people – No relationships like ours any more. Unless you're threesomes, you're not doing it.

STEPH. Where d'you get that from?

MAX. Adverts. Dunno. *Skins* and that.

STEPH. That's telly.

MAX. Agh…

STEPH. Did you talk to him? About the masturbation?

MAX. Masturb – We talk old. Our son's a wanker from a long line of wankers, not to be ashamed of.

Beat.

STEPH. He's a good boy, isn't he?

MAX. So hot, everything's melting.

Beat.

STEPH. Come on, why don't we open that Lambrini we've been saving?

MAX. On a school night?

They stand.

STEPH. Why not?

DANI, FITZ *and* WHEELER *are stood in the brakelights of the car.*

FITZ. You're gonna have to reverse over it.

WHEELER. What?

FITZ. It's not dead.

WHEELER. How do you know it's not dead?

FITZ. You can see it breathing.

DANI. The vet could save it.

FITZ. The twenty-four-hour helicopter vet? Yeah, probably. Just get back in and slam it into reverse.

WHEELER. I'm not doing it, you do it.

FITZ. Wheeler, that fox is dying slow.

WHEELER. What if I only get it a bit?

DANI. It's still breathing.

WHEELER (*to* DANI). Get in the car, babe.

DANI. Help it.

WHEELER. Babe, get in the car –

> FITZ *stamps on the fox seven times, furiously and with random timing.*

FITZ. Which way's home?

WHEELER. Dun't be stupid.

FITZ. Stoopud? For getting you out of suffin' again? Weren't stoopud when you'd get kicked out of class and I'd walk with ya, get in a fight and I'd pile in – funny then, weren't it? Cos Fitz is mental, take anything on, Fitz – You know what's funnier? Fitz revising. Hilarious. Goin' home.

DANI. You can't go home, you don't know where you are.

TWO. All around them's the same view.

ONE. Flat fields.

> FITZ *tries a different route.*

> More flat fields.

FITZ. Sake!

FITZ *gives up and sits.*

DANI *is staring at the dead animal.*

DANI. We had a dog this colour. Held his head when they put him down and his eyes just – (*Gestures expanding pupils.*) Like you could fall in. Mum's like, 'Don't touch. Unhygienic, Daniella, not hygienic.' She's an artist. My mother. Ursula. Ursula's an *artiste*. My dad left and, I see her, at night, probably not sleepwalking but in the garden… All…

Giggling, DANI *imitates her mother walking.*

Like she's lost something. Watches me sleep sometimes, thinks I can't see her with her eyes all… like the dog's. Come on, Fitz, it's only a little further. Please? Pretty please?

FITZ *stands up.*

STEPH. The little shit! I've taught him to leave messages if he goes out. It's the same as his indicating, he never indicates before he turns. I've taught him to leave messages.

MAX. You remember when we were his age? We were already planning our wedding.

STEPH. I'm talking about our missing son.

MAX. He'll be fine.

STEPH. Why have you got your shoes on?

MAX. I decided to keep them on.

STEPH. It's you who says we take them off.

Beat.

You're leaving me.

MAX. No, it's just…

STEPH (*laughing in disbelief*). Oh my…

MAX. Do we still want this, Steph, or are we just… used to it?

STEPH. Are you leaving me?

MAX. No. I don't know. I don't want to. I'm –

STEPH. Drunk and full of weird chicken. And confused and it's late, saying things you don't mean.

MAX *begins to cry.*

MAX *wipes his nose with his sleeve.*

Not your sleeve, Max. Don't use your sleeve.

'We Are Your Friends' by Justice vs Simian kicks in. DANI *is in the backseat singing along,* FITZ *is riding shotgun,* WHEELER *drives.*

WHEELER. Whose house party is this, babe? Is it still gonna be –

DANI. Why're you calling me 'babe'?

WHEELER. Huh?

FITZ. How fast you going?

DANI (*looking back*). What's that?

WHEELER. Nothin'.

ONE. Police lights flicker in the mirror.

FITZ. That's not nothin' –

WHEELER. I weren't doing nothing illegal.

FITZ. 'Cept driving a stolen car.

WHEELER. They won't know about that.

DANI. You get police out here?

WHEELER. He's probably just trying to get past.

DANI. Why aren't you slowing down?

WHEELER. There's a passing place up here.

FITZ. Dun't be stoopud.

WHEELER (*looking at* FITZ). Stupid?

DANI. Slow down.

FITZ. Wheeler.

Siren.

WHEELER. One night, Fitz!

DANI. You're making it worse.

WHEELER. Will you take a risk with me for once?

FITZ. There's a bridge comin', Wheeler.

DANI. Stop the car, you dick!

WHEELER. I need a wingman, Fitz.

FITZ. There's a fucken bridge!

Sounds of an aeroplane ripping the air on take-off, then settling into BOB*'s computer simulation.*

TWO. It's two fifteen in the morning and Bob has been holding his course, keeping things safe, in a fug of burnt fish fingers. He's flying over the North Sea.

BOB *gradually angles the joystick down.*

BOB. I 'on't care.

RECORDED VOICE. Flight 274 from Johannesburg, you are off-course, repeat, off-course.

BOB. Passengers have been evacuated, now leave me be, wun't ya?

TWO. He's coming in low towards the Suffolk coast.

An alarm sounds.

RECORDED VOICE. Altitude, altitude, altitude – (*Repeats.*)

BOB. I'm gonna fucken – (*Farts.*) blow us all to…

RECORDED VOICE. Emergency! Emergency!

BOB. Air traffic control, I'm completely…

TWO. He can see the simulated shadow on the computer screen of a Boeing 747 plummeting towards the roof of his small terraced home in Reydon.

BOB. …completely broked.

An explosion.

WHEELER. We're fine. We're gonna be fine. I didn't lose control, he'll just wonder... just ask –

COBB *stands at the driver's window.*

COBB. Ha' ya got your driving licence an' unsurance docamentation, please?

WHEELER. I'm sorry 'bout the headlight, we hit a fox.

COBB. Ha' ya got your driving licence an' unsurance docamentation, please?

WHEELER. It's at home at the moment.

Beat.

COBB. Been drinkin' anoit?

WHEELER. Noooo. Designated driver.

COBB. Spoose you din't hear nor see the sirens on the police vehicle for the last thousand meters or so?

WHEELER *smiles.*

Step outside the car, please.

WHEELER. Oh God. (*To* DANI *and* FITZ.) Stay there.

WHEELER *gets out of the car.*

DANI. Fitz... What's he gonna say?

Beat.

Fitz, this can't happen to me.

Beat.

I can't just be 'promising', Fitz, it doesn't mean anything unless I go on to a good college. If I get arrested because you and your friend got horny and stupid – ! (*Giggling.*) I'm sorry. I must sound really... You're a bit cheeky, though, get the odd black mark and it doesn't mean as much... You could tell him that I didn't know you were under age or that this wasn't your car – ?

FITZ. Beg me.

DANI. Sorry?

FITZ. That's all so easy for you, in't it?

Beat.

DANI. Is this cos I kissed Wheeler?

FITZ gets more comfortable in his seat.

Course I'll beg you. I'm begging you, okay? Can you help me now, please?

Beat.

FITZ gets out of the car.

Bleep.

URSULA *(into the phone)*. It's almost three a.m., Dani. I'm sure you're fine, there's food, I made your bed, fresh sheets, it's really quite late now and you should be at home – WHERE ARE YOU? No, you're grown up now, but grown-ups have responsibilities not to… You scare me, Daniell-Dani, and I know I'm not good with intimacy or – or bonding, I know you prefer your father, but… I don't want a huggy-mummy relationship, I just… We used to – When you were tiny and purple, I didn't think I'd know how to hold you but… when I did, your hand… Ever so slightly, you gripped me… We did used to hold each other. *(Beat.)* Stupid.

URSULA presses a button.

RECORDED VOICE. Message deleted. To leave a message press –

URSULA hangs up.

FITZ is signing something.

COBB. Steven's fine, 'To Steven', if that's okay? Couple a years and that autograph'll be worth a bit, I reckon.

FITZ gives him the signed piece of paper.

FITZ. Cheers, Cobby.

COBB. PC Cobb whilst I'm on duty, Fitzo, yeah? This one always try an' outrun the coppas, do he?

FITZ. My idea, reckoned we'd see if them drivin' courses work for ya.

COBB. Cheek. Now, dun't get in no trouble, orlroit? And take more of them direct free-kicks, in't renewing the season ticket if you dun't.

COBB *exits*.

DANI *shoves* WHEELER.

DANI. You twat! You complete and utter fucking twat!

Beat.

Thanks for that, Fitz. I can walk from here, thank you, I'm going to my house party, so, you can fuck off to your back-water villages.

DANI *leaves*.

FITZ. In't this the bit where you say thanks? Wingman?

WHEELER. Why you being such a dick?

FITZ. Why you being such a dick?

WHEELER. This about her? About a girl? Oh, like suffin' woulda happened between you two anyway.

FITZ. What's that mean?

WHEELER. This is the world, Fitz, natural selection, hard wall of fact, alright? People get hurt and get over things. There'll be more girls at this party, anyway. I in't driving home 'til I've at least seen it. You coming or pussying out?

WHEELER *and* FITZ *head to the party*.

MAX *is holding a joint*.

STEPH. Max! Is that what I think it is? Where'd you get that?

MAX. Scott's room, few days ago.

STEPH. Should we call that number, that 'FRANK' number? We can't talk to him about drugs, we just did the wank talk. We could buy some books and leave them out.

MAX. I don't know, he's sixteen, maybe this is normal.

STEPH. Well… we can't give it him back.

STEPH *lights the joint*.

MAX. What are you doing?

Beat.

Can I have a go?

STEPH. You don't smoke. You've never smoked anything.

MAX. Exactly.

STEPH *passes the joint to* MAX.

MAX *smokes awkwardly*.

Beat.

WHEELER. Must get in round the back, come on.

TWO. It's a half hour before dawn, the night's at its darkest.

'My Baby Just Cares for Me' by Nina Simone is playing inside the house.

WHEELER. This is gonna be heavy! We'll just get in there and… What?

FITZ. I 'on't think I want your help tomorrow.

WHEELER. What?

FITZ. I in't gonna stay on.

WHEELER. I'm sorry I kissed her, it was a cock-block, but it just happened –

FITZ. This in't about that.

WHEELER. You're not even gonna try?

FITZ. You know I'm not clever enough to git into sixth form, I know I in't.

WHEELER. You're clever enough. You're clever enough.

FITZ. I 'on't want to then.

WHEELER. What about your future, you know, your –

FITZ. I'll work suffin' out.

WHEELER. Gonna bind revision books for other people your whole life? What about – We're homeboys, I mean –

FITZ. I got with Chloë. I got with Chloë when you were last away.

WHEELER. My Chloë?

FITZ. Yeah.

WHEELER. When I was in Mexico?

FITZ *nods*.

I bought you a sombrero.

FITZ. You think everyone's so stoopud. Think she didn't know you were cheating on her? You had crabs, had to git herself sorted –

WHEELER. Why're you telling me this?

FITZ (*shrugs*). Squeezing, getting the poison out –

WHEELER. What'd you do?

FITZ. You can still call me a virgin, din't have sex.

WHEELER. D'you lick her out?

FITZ (*shrugging*). We were wasted.

WHEELER. Fuck you. She go down on you? Don't answer that, don't… Where was this, where'd it happen?

FITZ. Her bed.

WHEELER. With the… the balloons on the duvet cover? The – What underwear?

FITZ. Don't remember.

WHEELER (*beginning to cry, voice breaking, twisting his hair*). Was it white with little hearts? Was it the stuff I bought her? With little – You're my best friend! My best…

Beat.

FITZ. Fuck's sake, Wheels.

WHEELER *suddenly wipes his face and composes himself.*

WHEELER. Nah, this is… This'll be… We'll go in, see if this party's any good, then…

WHEELER *looks at* FITZ.

TWO. It's half four and the sunrise is already fading out the stars as Max and Steph finish the pizza.

MAX (*mouth full*). Hawaiian.

STEPH. Can't believe I'm still hungry.

MAX. Mmmm.

STEPH. Do you think that weed was Afghan?

MAX. Mmmm – What?

Beat.

I'm sorry I've been crap.

STEPH. You haven't been crap.

MAX. I've been crap.

STEPH. I've never thanked you, have I? For every time you've come to bed later than me and brought two glasses of water. I've meant to.

MAX. You've got… (*Giggly.*) On your top… Tomato all down your top, and pineapple, what have you been doing, rubbing yourself with it?

STEPH *picks it off her top and eats it.*

Ergh!

STEPH. Want some?

They get the giggles.

DANI *cues 'Crimson and Clover' by Tommy James and The Shondells.* DANI *dances alone.*

ONE. Not far from where the boys parked the car, Blakeney's premiere holiday home, Dani has found her father's old Dansette record player.

TWO. Dani has scanned every picture on every wall, desk and bedside table. From every image, the other family, the two boys and their mother, grin at her from beside her father.

DANI. Not one picture. Not a single picture of Mum or of me...

TWO. Fitz and Wheeler walk over the broken glass of the French doors, past the deckchair that was thrown through them, into the open-plan kitchen.

Beat.

DANI. My dad used to play me this, vinyl. Can't believe it still works.

FITZ. D'you smash the window-door thing?

DANI (*pouring shots*). Why did the Mexican push his wife off the cliff?

WHEELER. It's, like, five in the morning, Dani –

DANI. Used to surprise me, back from work early, wait in the kitchen – AH!

WHEELER. We shouldn't be here.

DANI. Drink these or you'll just fall asleep, loser.

WHEELER. This isn't a house party, Dani, it's just an empty house –

DANI. Why did the Mexican push his wife off the cliff?

WHEELER. It's over, alright? Let's just go –

FITZ. I 'on't know, why did the Mexican push his wife off the cliff?

DANI. Tequila!

FITZ *and* DANI *do a shot.* WHEELER *does his last.*

Round the world, where to next? Ouzo, sambuca –

WHEELER *kisses* DANI. *She stops him by laughing in the middle of it.*

Come on, dance, dance...

DANI *breaks from* WHEELER *to dance to the song.*

Fitz? (*Dancing with* FITZ*'s hands in hers*.) Mum dances to this alone sometimes, mourning Dad even though he's still alive... Dance with me!

WHEELER. It's one thing nicking a car, but this is –

DANI *kisses* WHEELER *whilst holding onto* FITZ.

(*Breaking away*.) Fuck this, fuck it, no.

DANI. We have a drop-out!

WHEELER. Yeah, I'm dropping out, I don't wanna do this any more.

DANI *starts smashing things*.

FITZ. What ya doing – ?

DANI. Ooh, morals.

FITZ. What's wrong with ya?

DANI *hits* FITZ.

DANI. Why'd you always start on bouncers? Is it an interesting problem?

WHEELER. Dani.

Giggling, DANI *repeatedly hits* FITZ.

DANI. Is it so they hit you? So you feel it outside instead of in? Hit me! Want me to take the piss, abuse your dead mum? Doesn't mean you're more – You're not better – Fucking hit me!

FITZ *grabs* DANI *violently,* DANI *rages and struggles, still laughing*.

You can't even hurt me properly, you pansy –

DANI *realises that she is crying as* FITZ *and* DANI *fold into a hug*.

WHEELER *watches*.

ONE. In Walberswick, Ursula has crawled into the fresh sheets of her daughter's bed and stared at the resolutely blank screen of her mobile phone. No messages. No texts.

URSULA. Bloody thing! Bloody fucking shitting… (*Throws phone*.)

ONE. It's when trying to cry, that Ursula notices the glow-in-the-dark stars that they had stuck to the bedroom ceiling.

URSULA *smiles, almost giggles*.

The fact that they're not in the correct constellations is exactly the kind of thing that would piss Dani's father off.

Sounds of the sea.

FITZ. What you doing?

WHEELER. Come near me and I'll… (*Shakes his head*.)

ONE. Wheeler's left Fitz and Dani in the house and has walked into the sea, little waves lap at his knees.

FITZ. There's a riptide, Wheeler, dun't –

WHEELER. Why you here?

Beat.

FITZ. She called her mum. She's getting picked up.

WHEELER. I've been trying to help you get out, get over…

FITZ. I in't a piece of your coursework.

WHEELER. I'm gonna swim, just disappear, swim away –

FITZ. No deeper.

WHEELER. Like I'd want rescuing from you.

FITZ. Let's git the car back, yeah?

WHEELER. Get the car back? What you talkin' about?

FITZ. We wouldn't of got away from Cobby. The door weren't broken, you didn't hotwire it. I dunno how it was in Lowestoft, but it's your dad's work car, in't ut? Lie to yourself so much, you believe it. 'Bout this, your urban moosic – look where you're from! 'Bout me, and if I give a fuck 'bout crustaceans and croissants –

WHEELER. I knew they were hot. Saw you heat the scissors up, we're in English together, Fitz, that wasn't pretending, that was real, for life.

FITZ. I just want different things to you, they in't worse, my dad, my home –

WHEELER. Your dad thinks farting is a condition, he's a hypochondriac, thinks everything's a illness –

FITZ. I know what it mean.

WHEELER *takes* FITZ's *face in his hands.*

WHEELER. If I heated them up, if I heated a pair of scissors to white-hot now, would you do it?

FITZ. Wheeler.

WHEELER. Would you take the scissors, if I heated them up, and get a scar – ?

FITZ *pushes* WHEELER *off.*

FITZ. Y'oughta git back for Biology.

WHEELER. You fucken –

FITZ *and* WHEELER *collide and are consumed by the water.*

TWO. As much as Wheeler holds Fitz under, he holds himself under.

ONE. They tumble, disorientated.

TWO. Every fracture in their friendship, their history –

ONE. Every classroom cut-down –

TWO. All rushing through their heads –

ONE. Saltwater burns their eyes, nose –

TWO. Compressing their lungs –

ONE. Squeezing them –

TWO. Can't be under much longer –

ONE. No longer –

Exploding from the water, FITZ punches WHEELER twice, hard.

FITZ. I in't another you… I 'on't want what you want – What's wrong with staying here?

WHEELER. I've only been trying to help.

FITZ. People get over stuff their own way.

WHEELER. I'm driving home.

They both get in the car in silence.

ONE. The boys pass Dani lighting a cigarette on the doorstep of the house. Turning the first corner, Fitz catches a glimpse of either the sunrise or a flame as the house disappears from the wing mirror.

TWO. The car settles into the commuter traffic, neither of them mention the police cars and fire engines heading in the opposite direction.

ONE. They know now, that although they might nod at each other at Christmas Eve or New Year's, they will be on opposite sides of the pub.

TWO. Arriving home, Fitz finds a note from his dad on his bed.

BOB. Gone a work. Pooter game's in the oven. Gonna do a bit more from now on, you're a gud lad.

TWO. Fitz notices all of the spelling mistakes, but decides –

FITZ. That's just how he spell 'em.

ONE. At home, Wheeler posts the keys through the letterbox and catches the bus to school for the last time.

WHEELER *opens his penknife, pushes his exam paper out of the way, and begins to engrave the table.*

TWO. It's ten a.m.

'Cold Days from the Birdhouse' by The Twilight Sad begins to play.

ONE. You have one-and-a-half hours, please don't forget to read the instructions carefully and ensure your name and student ID are in the correct fields on the cover sheet.

TWO. Wheeler's penknife is still razor-sharp.

ONE. An invigilator marks Fitz, otherwise known as Carl Stracchan, absent.

TWO. He's carving two names into the table.

ONE. GCSE Biology students, please turn over your papers, you may begin.

TWO. Deep in the desk, deep as on a gravestone.

WHEELER (*finishing his carving*). 'Fitz and Wheeler. The end.'

WHEELER *repositions his exam paper. Pulls out a pen and begins. The song plays out.*

The End.

A Nick Hern Book

I Caught Crabs in Walberswick first published in Great Britain in 2008 as a paperback original by Nick Hern Books Limited, 14 Larden Road, London W3 7ST, in association with Eastern Angles and HighTide

Cover image: Rob Devereux
Cover design: Ned Hoste, 2H

Typeset by Nick Hern Books, London
Printed and bound in Great Britain by CPI Antony Rowe, Chippenham, Wiltshire

A CIP catalogue record for this book is available from the British Library

ISBN 978 1 84842 038 0